How to be brilliant at
BALLET

Craig Dodd

FRANKLIN WATTS

This edition 2009

First published in 2007
by Franklin Watts

Copyright © Franklin Watts 2007
Franklin Watts
338 Euston Road
London NW1 3BH

Franklin Watts Australia
Level 17/207 Kent Street
Sydney, NSW 2000

Series editor: Jeremy Smith
Designer: Jason Billin

All photographs from the author's collection, apart from those listed below.

Alamy: 4b, 5t, 6-7 all, 8t, 16c, 22b, 26b. Corbis: 25r, 26t.

A CIP catalogue record for this book
is available from the British Library.

Dewey no: 792.8

ISBN: 978 0 7496 9345 9

Printed in China

Franklin Watts is a division of Hachette Children's Books,
an Hachette UK company.
www.hachette.co.uk

Learning ballet is a pleasure but like any form of physical exercise, it has an element of risk. Never try and perform complicated ballet moves without the supervision of your teacher.

Types of ballet

All ballet dancers learn basic steps but it is the choreographer who puts all these steps together to make a ballet. Some choreographers may want to create a straightforward Classical ballet. Britain's Sir Frederick Ashton (1904-88) made ballets to his own stories or retold fairy tales such as *Cinderella*. Other choreographers may just use just ballet steps with no story at all. These ballets are called Neo-Classical ballets. The American choreographer, George Balanchine, (1904-83) produced these kind of ballets. Finally, some choreographers, such as Jirí Kilián (b.1947), expect dancers to turn pure, classical steps into odd, but beautiful, shapes. This is called Modern Classical ballet.

Neo-Classical ballet

Modern Classical ballet

Ballet history

History is very important in the world of ballet. Every basic ballet move has been passed down from person to person over the centuries. Young dancers starting out on professional careers will spend a lot of their time dancing the classic ballets such as *Swan Lake* or *Sleeping Beauty*, which were created in Russia at the end of the 19th century.

An engraving showing the Ballet Comique de la Reine.

A painting of the Paris Opera Rue Richelieu, *from the 16th century.*

The first ballet

Ballet began as a court entertainment, brought to France by the Italian Catherine de Medici in the early 16th century when she married King Henri II of France. Ballet then was nothing like the ballet we know today. Ballets were entertainments that lasted for three or four days and involved animals, clowns, acrobats and lots of food and drink for the performers and audience. The *Ballet Comique de la Reine* of 1581 lasted six hours, and is thought to be the first recorded ballet.

French ballet

Catherine de Medici had three sons who each became king of France, one after the other. The last of her sons to take the throne was Louis XIV, who loved dancing so much that he started a ballet school in 1661. From this small beginning grew the world-famous Paris Opera Ballet. The Paris Opera Ballet school developed most of the positions of the feet and arms and the ways the body is held during ballet. This is why the words for these positions are all in French.

BALLET FACT

The *corps de ballet* is the name given to the dancers in a ballet company who do not dance by themselves but dance as a group. Above these dancers are the soloists, while at the top is the *Prima Ballerina* (males are called Principal Dancers) who dances all the lead and solo roles.

Russian ballet

In Russia, at the same time that Louis XIV was on the French throne, Tsar Peter the Great wanted his courtiers to do everything in the French style. They even spoke French in the Russian court. So Peter introduced ballet dancing to Russia. This was the beginning of the greatest ballet tradition of them all, based in Moscow and St Petersburg.

British and American ballet

The British and American schools of ballet are very new compared to French and Russian ballet. British ballet really only started in the 1930s, although ballets were performed in the UK by foreign companies such as Diaghilev's *Ballet Russes de Monte Carlo* before this. American ballet established itself from 1940 onwards.

The famous Russian ballerina Anna Pavlova (1881-1931).

Bolshoi ballet

Kirov ballet

DID YOU KNOW

There are two great Russian ballet companies: the Bolshoi and the Kirov. Bolshoi means 'big' in Russian and the company is certainly that – it has over 400 dancers performing at home in Moscow and abroad at any one time. The smaller Kirov company is based in St Petersburg. It was named after a murderous Communist chief, who died in 1934. The company's original name was Maryinsky and this name is now coming back into use.

Getting started

You don't have to look like a ballet dancer to learn ballet – the important thing is to want to learn. Look at some of the exercises and positions in this book and if you think you would like to learn more, then join a class. A good teacher will put you into a class that suits your experience (or lack of it!) and level of fitness. As you go to more and more classes, your 'ballet muscles' will develop and grow, and you will start to feel like a real ballet dancer.

Finding a school

Most towns have ballet schools run by enthusiastic, well-qualified teachers. The first and most important thing to consider is the teacher. Go and watch a couple of classes and see how well the teacher and pupils work together. Many retired dancers may not have as many qualifications as others, but the experience that they pass on can count for more than passing exams.

Boys and girls at the barre at a local ballet school.

The right music

Many schools use recorded music in their classes. This can be turned on and off, rewound or fast-forwarded in an instant and many different types of music can be used. Some ballet schools use a pianist who can play fast or slow, soft or loud, waltz or march, usually without being told. Changing tempo (speed), using different tunes and playing jolly music that has nothing to do with the ballet are all part of the art of music for a ballet class.

Choosing clothes

You will need smart but simple practice clothes. Black tights and a white T-shirt is usual for boys. Light pink tights and a leotard with an optional chiffon skirt are usual for girls. Many schools have their own uniforms, but they are never very different from these basics. Properly fitted shoes are vital – they must be flat and flexible and secured with elastic or ribbons – and long hair should be tied back.

Clothing for girls

Clothing for boys

TOP TIP

Look at the floor. A beautiful old wooden floor can look marvellous, but if the wood has been laid on concrete it will have no 'give'. Jumps will end in a thud, which is bad for your knees and hips and will lead to injuries. A good modern floor supplied by one of the dance-floor specialists is always best. You don't literally have to bounce off it, but when you land you should feel 'happy'. So ask about the floor before you sign up for classes.

The five positions – feet

Have a go at placing your feet in the five positions.
Match your feet to the photographs.

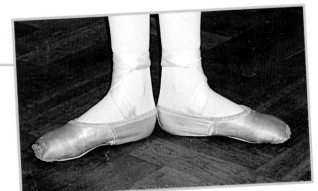

1. First position

Keep your legs together with your heels
touching and your feet pointing in
opposite directions to form a straight line.

Hint: Keep your back straight.

2. Second position

This position looks like first position but
with your feet about one and a half times
the length of your foot apart. Only you can
work that out.

Hint: Make sure that your arms and body
weight are evenly balanced.

3. Third position

You bring your feet together, one behind the
other, in third position. The heel of one foot
should fit into the instep of the other one.
This should be a comfortable and natural
movement, although you will probably have
wobbly moments, especially as the matching
arms (see pages 12-13) are not balanced as
they were with first and second positions.

Hint: Think of yourself as a letter X as your
legs are now crossed and your arms are not
equally positioned (one is up and the other
one is down). You must keep control of your
waist in order to keep your balance.

TOP TIP

It is very important to get third
position correct because then you
stand a much better chance of getting
the all-important fifth position right.

4. Fourth position

Fourth position is a mixture of all the other positions so far. The easiest way to do fourth position is to put your feet into first position and then slide one foot forward by about 30 centimetres (the length of a school ruler).

Hint: In this position, resist the temptation to put too much weight on one foot.

5. Fifth position

Fifth position is what everyone is aiming for. It looks easy – just one foot completely behind the other with feet pointing in the opposite directions – but try it! It is not easy! Fifth position is the starting point for every great turn or jump, so you can't be a ballet dancer if you can't do fifth.

Hint: Keep trying. Don't force the position. It will slide into place one day.

DID YOU KNOW

Doing the five positions of the feet can help with turn out (see page 15). But as Dame Ninette de Valois (1898-2001), founder of London's Royal Ballet said, 'He's got no feet and hers are like pats of butter.' She was describing two of the greatest dancers of the last century, the Australian Robert Helpmann (1909-86) and Britain's Margot Fonteyn (see page 4).

The five positions – arms

For each of the five feet positions there are five arm positions. The arm positions are called *ports de bras* – this means 'the way you hold your arms' in French. The arm positions are very natural and should not be forced.

TOP TIP

For ballet dancers, the 'line' of the arm starts at the fingertips. It then follows through a naturally curved elbow to an elegant neck and well placed head.

1. First position

In first position curve both of your arms down naturally in front of you with the fingers just a few centimetres apart to give a rounded shape. This is called *bras bas* or 'low arms'.

2. Second position

In second position hold your arms out to the side at a natural shoulder height, with no nasty angles at the elbows.

3. Third position

This position mixes positions one and two – place one arm in first and the other in second.

4. Fourth position

In fourth position place one arm in second and raise the other arm above your head. This dancer has moved her head - try not to do this when getting into fourth position.

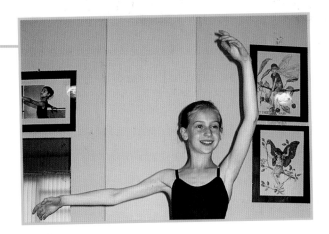

5. Fifth position

To do fifth position, raise both of your arms above your head in a nicely rounded shape. Technically this is called *en couronne*, which means 'making a crown' in French.

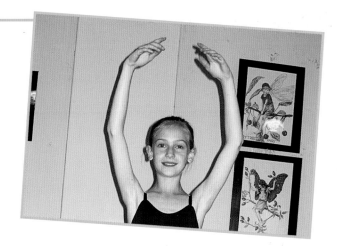

Below is a summary of the five positions, showing feet and arms together.

1.

2.

3.

4.

5.

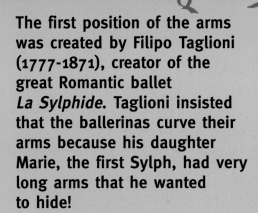

BALLET FACT

The first position of the arms was created by Filipo Taglioni (1777-1871), creator of the great Romantic ballet *La Sylphide*. Taglioni insisted that the ballerinas curve their arms because his daughter Marie, the first Sylph, had very long arms that he wanted to hide!

A ballet class

Every ballet dancer, whether they are six years old or 60, amateur or professional, does the same kind of exercises and positions in their classes. All ballet classes follow the same basic structure so that the dancers' muscles warm up at the right rate, enabling them to do more and more difficult exercises as the class goes on. Ballet classes allow dancers to perfect their moves and to develop their own style.

Floor work

Many of the first exercises you do at ballet school are on the floor so that your back has firm support and there is no danger of falling and injuring yourself. Teachers usually start very young students off with simple stretching exercises that involve sitting with the legs straight out, pointing the toes as far as they will go then pulling the feet back to a 90-degree angle with the heels just off the floor. In children's ballet classes this is called the 'good toes, bad toes' exercise.

Barre work

Next, you perform exercises standing at the barre. The barre is a long, narrow wooden pole mounted on the wall about adult waist height. Rest your hand on the barre for support but try not to grip it hard as this will make your body tense and your movements less graceful.

Centre studio work

Finally you will repeat barre exercises in the centre of the studio without any support at all. By repeating barre exercises without the barre, ballet dancers learn to fine-tune their balance and build up their confidence for jumps and other steps.

Turn out

During all the floor and barre exercises dancers must remember to 'turn out' their hips – not just their knees and ankles. It is not as strange an idea as it seems. If you stand normally, feet forward, you can only dance facing the audience or sideways and are unable to do big jumps diagonally across the stage. Standing normally ballerinas cannot perform the beautiful extensions of the legs, known as *arabesques* (see page 23), among many other steps.

TOP TIP

Pretending to be a frog will help your turn out. Get down on all fours and slide down as far as you can into a split position with your knees bent. Tense your muscles for 20 seconds and to the count of 1-2-3-4-5 try to slide down towards the floor till you rest on the floor. Keep the body flat on the floor, the hips square and the knees in line with the hips.

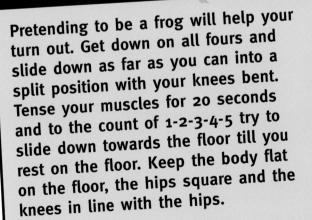

DID YOU KNOW

In the 1820s, the Italian Carlos Blasis created the five positions of the feet to make the turn out of the hips easier. He based his movements on the fancy way royal courtiers walked.

Perfect *pliés*

After warming up on the floor, dancers move to the wall of the studio to work at the barre. The first exercise they do is the *plié*.

The basic move

Pliés are the basis of almost every ballet move that is done at the barre, in the centre of the studio or on stage. *Plié* means 'to bend' in French. *Pliés* give you the bounce you need for jumps and they provide preparation for turns.

A plié at the barre.

Do a plié

To do a *plié*, hold the barre lightly for support. Do not grip it. All you have to do is slowly bend your knees outwards while lowering your body. Keep your back straight and your hips level. Don't let your bottom stick out! This movement should be smooth and even. Look at the picture on the left to see how to sweep your free arm through the movement. You can do *pliés* in every one of the five feet positions (see pages 10 and 11). While doing a *plié* move your arms through the five arm positions (see pages 12-13) as smoothly as possible.

TOP TIP

Throughout a *plié* concentrate on keeping the weight of your body evenly distributed over both feet.

Different types of *plié*

There are two types of *plié*: *demi-pliés* (half knee bends) where you lower your body halfway to the floor by bending at the knee, and *grands pliés* (full knee bends) where you continue down to the floor so that your bottom almost rests on your heels (which should be raised off the floor).

demi-pliés

BALLET FACT

Every dancer wants a solo role, but some young dancers dread being cast for the opening of *Etudes*, a ballet by Harold Lander (1905-71). The opening involves the solo ballerina doing a *grand plié* with the feet in fifth position to a simple ballet class tune. It may sound easy but in front of a full opera house, under a spotlight, even the best dancers can get a bad case of the wobbles.

grands pliés

Stretching and stepping

Now you can move on to more complicated movements at the barre. There are lots of barre exercises but we will concentrate on *battements tendus* and *grands battements*. When doing the positions on this page concentrate on placing your arms and legs in the correct positions and try to relax your shoulders.

Students practise battements tendus.

Stretching steps

Battements tendus means 'stretched beatings' in French. This sounds a lot worse than it is! *Tendus* means that you must stretch your leg and foot across the floor without letting your foot leave the floor – it should just lightly sweep across it. These exercises are designed to make your feet stronger and to use all the muscles in your legs. Practise your *tendus* in preparation for more complicated footwork called *allegro* (meaning 'fast' in Italian) later on.

BALLET FACT

The leg closest to the barre is called the supporting leg. The other leg is called the working leg – it is the leg that does all the work performing the movements of the exercise.

Grand battements. *The working leg is whisked off the floor into the air. Use your arms to help you balance your way through the exercise.*

Big beats

Grands battements are also called 'big beats'. They are exercises that improve a dancers balance and strength – essential for jumping.

1. To do a 'big beat' stand at the barre with your feet in fifth position (see pages 10-13).

2. Keeping your working leg straight, move it quickly off the floor into the air, to above waist height (if you can!).

3. Let your leg come back down to the floor, keeping control all the time. When your working leg comes down to the floor your foot should be at an angle so that your heel, not your toe, touches the floor first.

4. Raise your leg up to the side in the same movement you have just performed to the front and again control the return to the floor.

inding a balance

of the steps described here are
vays repeated on 'both sides' –
st with your right hand on the
rre and then, after turning
und, with your left hand on the
rre. Always doing exercises on
th sides ensures that a dancer's
uscles are working equally, left
d right. It also compensates for
e fact that some dancers
turally turn to the left and
hers to the right.

Practise these steps first with your right hand on the barre, then with your left.

Circles and bends

Once you have used the barre to perform *pliés* and other steps, you can then use it to make circles and 'unfold' your legs.

Making a circle

In *ronds de jambes à terre* (meaning 'circular movement of the leg on the ground' in French) you draw a circle on the floor with your working leg. First, stand at the barre with your working leg in second position. Point your foot. Circle your foot round to the back of your body, keeping your toe on the floor at all times. Move your foot forward to the front of your body, keeping your toes pointed but your foot flat along the floor. Point your foot to the front and then circle back round to where you started.

Performing ronds de jambes à terre *at the barre.*

Performing ronds de jambes en l'air.

In the air

Now work your way through *ronds de jambes en l'air* – a circular movement of the leg in the air. You will need to stand at the barre and make the same shape with your working leg as you did in *ronds de jambes à terre* but this time raise your leg to make a circle in the air with just the bottom half of it (this means from your knee to your toes).

DID YOU KNOW

The biggest ballet class in the world took place on 12 October 2003, when 530 ballet dancers from 41 schools took a class at the barre in a shopping centre in Cape Town, South Africa. The youngest ballet dancer was ten, the oldest was 52.

Time to unfold

Next comes the *développés*, which means 'to unfold'.

1. Stand at the barre with your feet in fifth position. Trace a line up your leg with your pointed toe to just below the knee.

2. Once you have moved your leg up to the side (above left) or to the back or front, unfold your leg (above), then slowly allow it to move back down to the floor to close back into fifth position.

TOP TIP

As you get to the end of the barre exercises it is important to keep moving – don't stop or your muscles will cool down. Do some relaxing stretching exercises – for example those shown in the picture on the left. Put on a sweatshirt or a jumper so that you keep warm for the centre studio work to come.

Centre studio

Now you are ready to move away from the barre and work in the middle of the dance studio or space. You have to feel confident to work in the centre of the studio because you don't have the barre to support you. You are on your own. It is important to start slowly and work your way up to concentrating on holding poses in perfect balance.

Dancers practise adage jumps

Start slowly

You start with *adage* steps. *Adage* comes from the Italian word *adagio*, which means 'slow' or 'at ease'. The idea is that you slowly get used to your new position in the studio. You are now free to use both of your arms as you are not holding on to the barre. You will start with small jumps (shown above) and move on to bigger ones. But centre studio work is not all jumping around.

The attitude position

Stand on one foot with the other leg raised and bent at the knee behind you. This pose is based on a famous statue of Mercury by Giovanni da Bologna.

This girl is practicing the attitude position

DID YOU KNOW

The British record for an *entrechat* (see opposite) in the *Guinness Book of Records* is held by Wayne Sleep who managed ten changes of feet while in the air. This is a brilliant technical achievement that is of no use whatsoever, as the feet changes are performed so quickly that the audience can't count them!

Arabesque

Stand on one leg and raise the other high at the back, keeping your arms in line with the raised leg. There are many variations of the *arabesque*, but it is at its most glorious when performed by many ballerinas at once – seeing 32 ballerinas perform this all together in *La Bayadre* is one of the highlights of ballet art.

Advanced quick jumps

More advanced ballet moves include the *entrechat* (meaning 'braided' or 'interwoven') and the *fouetté* (meaning 'whipped'). In an *entrechat*, a male ballet dancer jumps up, twiddles his feet and lands in perfect fifth position. In a *fouetté*, the ballerina *on pointe* (see pages 24-25) uses her raised leg to whip around as many as 32 times. *Fouettés* are followed by *jetés*, big jumps from one foot to the other while throwing the working leg out to the side. You still have to point your feet throughout the jump, remembering all the time your *ports de bras* (see pages 12-13) and how to hold your head.

The entrechat *move is made up of three parts shown in the photographs on the right.*

Fifth position for take-off

In the air, with feet pointing downwards, change feet

Landing in fifth position, with the other leg in front

During a performance of Don Quixote, *the ballerina* fouettés *to impress the men.*

Three ballerinas perform grand jeté, *appearing to float in the air.*

En pointe

It is usually only ballerinas who go *en pointe*. This is one of the most beautiful moves in ballet, where ballerinas stand on the tip of their toes, perfectly balanced. But you should not attempt to go *en pointe* before your feet, ankles and back are strong enough to carry your weight.

A balancing act

Pointe shoes have solid toes. When a ballerina flips herself up onto these hard points, all her body weight is concentrated on the tips of her toes, rather than over the whole of her feet. This requires a fantastic sense of balance and a great deal of strength and skill.

A ballerina going on pointe.

Special shoes

Having the right shoes for *pointe* work is very important. If you are ready to go *en pointe* you will have to find a shoemaker who can specially fit your feet to pointe shoes. *Pointe* shoes come with separate ribbons, because you are the only person who knows how the ribbons fit and you must sew them on yourself.

REMEMBER

You must be over eight or nine years old before going *en pointe* because if you start too young, the bones in your feet can be harmed and you will end up not being able to dance at all. You must never go *en pointe* without the approval and supervision of a trained ballet teacher.

A perfect fit

How you sew on your ribbons, usually bought with the shoes, is very personal. Your shoemaker will tell you how to sew them and then it is up to you, no one else. When they are on, always make sure the small end pieces are tucked in. Some dancers like to 'break in' their shoes because they can be a bit stiff when new. This can mean softly bending them, walking about the house in them, or hitting them on concrete – depending on personal need! Experienced dancers with strong feet often take out the inner linings. This is not advised for less experienced dancers.

BALLET FACT

French ballet star Sylvie Guilleme (b.1965) and Britain's Darcy Bussell (b.1969) can both raise their right leg from a *développé* whilst standing en pointe to make 'six o'clock' position, with their right foot behind their right ear.

Darcy Bussell

DID YOU KNOW ?

There is an all-male ballet company called *Les Trocadero de Monte Carlo*. They all dance *en pointe* – not something that male ballet dancers usually do – and are a huge success all over the world.

Ballet boyz

Men in ballet have played different roles through the centuries. In the oldest ballets, men played women. Then they did nothing more than carry the Prima Ballerina around. At the very end of the 19th century came the great Russian dancer Vaslav Nijinsky (1890-1950). With his athletic ability and great technique, Nijinsky was a sensation, and had ballets created for him.

Vaslav Nijinsky in Petrouchka, *a tragic tale of a puppet who falls in love with a toy ballerina. The ballet is set to music by Igor Stravinsky.*

Inspiring Russians

More recently, in the 1960s, came Rudolf Nureyev (1938-93), a ballet dancer with outstanding technique. He escaped from Communist Russia and formed a famous partnership with Britain's Margot Fonteyn that extended her career by several years. Nureyev, and other Russians who followed him to the west, inspired many young men to take up ballet. Today male dancers are back in fashion, but in some countries, notably Russia and Denmark, they have never been out of fashion. In both of these countries, young men fight their way into ballet school, and can be found as Principal Dancers with most of the major ballet companies around the world.

Cuban connections

Cuba has probably produced more outstanding male dancers than any other country. One of them, Carlos Acosta (b.1973), is one of the greatest male dancers alive today. Acosta is a product of the Cuban Ballet School, founded and still directed by the Prima Ballerina Assoluta Alicia Alonso (b.1917). Carlos divides his time between the British Royal Ballet and the American Ballet Theatre and dances a huge range of Modern and Classical ballets. He can jump like an athlete, spin like a spinning top and charm an audience all at the same time.

Carlos Acosta

Dancing for two

Male dancers are not just employed as Principal Dancers. Many dance in the ranks with ordinary ballerinas, which is why learning to dance with a ballerina in class is so important. This is called *pas de deux*, which means 'a dance for two people'. Male dancers are expected to hold up a ballerina while she spins and turns, but they also need to be able to lift her high overhead, like a dead weight, so male ballet dancers have to be very strong. Lifting is made easier if the ballerina helps at the beginning with a little jump.

BALLET FACT

Male ballet dancers perform three main holds during a ballet: the supported balance, travelling lift and straight lift.

Supported balance: the ballerina goes *on pointe* and the male ballet dancer acts as a support, holding her hand or waist.

Travelling lift: the ballerina makes a jump into the male dancer's arms and the male dancer carries her and then puts her down, sometimes on the other side of the stage.

Straight lift: the male dancer throws the ballerina straight up into the air and catches her.

DID YOU KNOW

The first male dancer to jump into the air and turn four times from fifth position to fifth position was American Richard Cragun (b.1944) when he was dancing with the famous German Stuttgart Ballet in 1972. Ice-skaters had done it before that, but they have the advantage of a fast run in at high speed. Cragun did it from standing still.

Show time!

Apart from the fun of dancing all year round, there is the excitement of the annual school ballet show to look forward to. This can range from something improvised at the end of the studio to something much larger. The photographs on these pages come from the Debra Bradnum Ballet School show at the Shaw Theatre in London. Two performances sold out to eager friends and parents.

Right place, right time

Before a ballet performance, the atmosphere is always the same. Everyone is in a state of nerves, and backstage everyone is in the wrong place. To get around this, Debra devised a colour-coding system to create some order for her 200 students. It worked superbly. On the day, everyone (well, almost everyone) knew exactly where they should be at exactly the right time.

Create a character

The school show is important because it gives students something to work towards. The perfect show is not a whole ballet but a collection of different pieces to show off every talent at every grade. It is also a chance to create characters, which is not done in class – one minute a white rabbit in *Alice in Wonderland*, the next minute a sunflower in *Flower Garden*.

BALLET FACT

The Royal Ballet School at Covent Garden, London, can take as few as two students from its own school into its corps de ballet.

Show skills

There are many other benefits to ballet shows; everyone can join in making costumes, learning about lighting, helping with a bit of scenery or making a video of the show, front stage and back. Getting into full make-up and costumes is always fun because, again, it is not done in class.

On stage

Finally, there is nothing more exciting to every ballet dancer, from the youngest student to the oldest professional, than the magical words 'curtain up'.

BALLET FACT

There are eight grades in ballet, run by the Royal Academy of Dance. These are followed by vocational exams: Intermediate Foundation (11 years and over); Intermediate (12 years and over); Advanced Foundation (13 years and over); Advanced 1 (14 years and over); Advanced 2 (15 years and over); and finally the Solo Seal Award, which can only be taken by dancers who have passed the Advanced 2 exam with distinction.

Glossary

Adagio In music, *adagio* means 'slowly', whereas in ballet, the meaning refers to slow, unfolding movements.

Allegro Bright and brisk movements.

Arabesque (Literally: 'in Arabic fashion') The position of the body supported on one leg with the opposite leg (with the knee straight) extended behind the body.

Attitude A pose in which the dancer stands on one leg, with the other leg lifted behind (*derrière*) in front (*en avant*) or on the side (*à la seconde*) of the body with the knee bent at 120 degrees.

Battement A beating action of the extended or bent leg. There are two types of *battements*, *grands battements* and *petits battements*.

Bras Arms.

Corps Body.

Développé A movement when the working leg is first lifted to just below the waist, then develops to the front.

Entrechat 'Interweaving' or 'braiding'. A step of beating in which the dancer jumps into the air and rapidly crosses the legs before and behind each other, usually jumping from the fifth position and landing back in the fifth position.

Fouetté A term applied to a whipping movement of the leg that causes the body to spin.

Jambe Leg.

Jeté A jump from one foot to the other in which the working leg is brushed into the air and appears to have been thrown.

Plié A basic bending movement of the knees.

Port de bras Movement of the arms in a motion around the body.

Rondes de jambe Circles of the foot on the ground, or in the air with leg bent at the knee

Turn out A rotation of the hip joint that comes from the hips, causing the knee and foot to turn outwards, away from the centre of the body.

Find out more

Weblinks

www.dancing-times.co.uk
Website of Britain's biggest selling ballet magazine. It carries information on every leading school as well as interesting features and reviews. It is also available monthly at newsagents.

www.nureyev.org
The official website of the Nureyev Foundation.

http://info.royaloperahouse.org/
The official website of the Royal Ballet.

http://www.ballet.org.uk/
The official site of the English National Ballet.

http://www.northernballettheatre. co.uk/
The official site of the Northern Ballet Theatre, the main touring company in English ballet.

Sites for scholarships and grants

www.billyelliotthemusical.com
Backstage information about the film and show which started the current dance explosion. Look out for the Working Title/ Billy Elliot Awards, which are now being given to promising dancers.

www.yorkshireballetseminars.co.uk
Britain's leading summer school which takes place in York. The faculty is of major international teachers, with special coaching sessions by such great dancers as Sir Anthony Dowell. They award many grants for which there is fierce competition.

www.balletmasterclass.com
If you wish to venture abroad then Prague is the place. The summer school there is organised in London by the Czech ballerina of the English National Ballet. Teachers include such well-known ballerinas such as Maina Gielgud.

Some schools for those who want to take dance more seriously

www.royalballetschool.co.uk
The most famous ballet school in Britain for which there is limited entry and fierce competition. The Junior School is for boarders in the beautiful White Lodge in Richmond Park.

www.enbschool.org.uk
The school of English National Ballet enjoys a close relationship with the company being taught by the permanent staff with master classes by principals of the company. Graduates hope to join the company, but, as with the Royal Ballet, places are limited.

www.artsed.co.uk
A long established school which for years has provided the children for ENB's annual production of *The Nutcracker*. Great dancers such as Irek Mukhamadov and Matz Skoog (Former Director of ENB) are regular guest teachers.

www.elmhurstdance.co.uk
Now the official school of the Birmingham Royal Ballet, it benefits from an extensive purpose-built studio complex and a close relationship with BRB and its director, David Bintley.

Note to parents and teachers: Every effort has been made by the Publishers to ensure that these websites are suitable for children, that they are of the highest educational value, and that they contain no inappropriate or offensive material. However, because of the nature of the Internet, it is impossible to guarantee that the contents of these sites will not be altered. We strongly advise that Internet access is supervised by a responsible adult.

Index